Fictions from the Self

Friends with the . . .

Also by the Author

Fictions from the Self

Michael Burkard

W · W · Norton & Company

New York   London

Published simultaneously in Canada by Penguin Books Canada Ltd., 2801 John Street, Markham, Ontario L3R 1B4.
Printed in the United States of America.

The text of this book is composed in 10/12.5 Trump, with display type set in Trump. Composition and manufacturing by The Maple-Vail Book Manufacturing Group. Book design by Margaret M. Wagner.

First Edition

Library of Congress Cataloging-in-Publication Data
Burkard, Michael, 1947–
    Fictions from the self / Michael Burkard.
      p.   cm.
    I. Title.
PS3552.U718F54   1988
813'.54—dc19
                                          87–18747
                                          CIP

ISBN 0-393-02507-1

W. W. Norton & Company, Inc., 500 Fifth Avenue, New York, N.Y. 10110
W. W. Norton & Company Ltd., 37 Great Russell Street, London WC1B 3NU
1 2 3 4 5 6 7 8 9 0

Acknowledgment is made to the following magazines in which some of these poems first appeared. The American Poetry Review: *"Gin. White Out.," "The Shadows are Ripe," "Love's Tongue," "When the Sun Rises," "Eating on a Starlit Porch," "For Him," "Fictions from the Self," "Like a Receipt," "The Story of Marie," "Picture with No Past to It," "Eerie," "Series of Photographs (The Genus)," "The Man I Heard Of," "8 Hour Voyage"* and *"Breathless Storm."* The Black Warrior Review: *"I Entered a House"* and *"Strangely Insane."* Crazyhorse: *"There Is No Night."* Fiction International: *"A Stranger Leaves Me."* Ironwood: *"Mood Indigo," "Inside a Clock," "Mysteries," "At That River,"* and *"River Sister."* The Little Magazine: *"My Sister Is Not a Dollar," "In the Rain, in the Odd City," "Stoney Lonesome"* and *"Amnesia."* Pequod: *"White Envelope on Black Sweater," "Enigma"* and *"Sequence of the Horses."* Ploughshares: *"Little Final Sunlight," "Too Many Drops," "The Brothers"* and *"The World at Dusk."* Quarry: *"One Day."* Quarterly West: *"Secret Warning."* Rubicon: *"Murnau"* and *"Woman on a Train* (Le Mistral)." Shankpainter: *"The Fellatio House"* and *"Candle of the Poor."* The Sonora Review: *"Shadow from Breathing"* and *"The Song Is Passing like a Wave."* Telescope: *"Directly in Shadow," "Far Sight," "North and South," "A Study in Scarlet," "The Hour Hand,"* and *"Untitled (I wanted to love those . . .)."* and 2 Plus 2 (Switzerland): *"I Can Tell You I Was Very Sad to Receive Your Piece of Sentiment"* and *"The Three of Us Stones."* The following poems are forthcoming. The Paris Review: *"A Series of Judgements."* Willow Springs: *"Child at Anchor," "The Night Is a Sea,"* and *"To Rose."* Quarterly West: *"On a Train Approaching Midnight"* and *"Zane Grey."*

"Strangely Insane" and *"The Story of Marie"* also appear in New American Poets of the 80's, ed. Jack Meyers and Roger Weingarten (Green Harbor: Wampeter Press, 1984).

The epigraph from Rafael Alberti's poem "Harold Loyd, Estudiante," is from The Owl's Insomnia, *translated by Mark Strand, published by Antheneum, 1973, and is reprinted by permission of Atheneum and Mark Strand.*

"Milk Cow Blues" words and music by Kokomo Arnold © copyright 1934, 1963 by MCA Music Publishing, a division of MCA Inc., New York, NY 10022. Used by permission. All rights reserved.

The epigraph to the poem "Stoney Lonesome" is from the poem "Follow the Drinking Gourd" by Robert Creeley, from Pieces, Charles A. Scribner and Sons, Inc. 1969, *and is reprinted by permission of Charles A. Scribner and Sons.*

The line, "On a train approaching midnight," in the poem "After a Line by Louis Simpson," is taken from Simpson's poem, "Baruch" in Searching for the OX, William Morrow *and Company, Inc., 1976, and is reprinted by permission of William Morrow and Company.*

for Mary Alice Johnston

¿Fuiste tú la que tuvo la culpa de la lluvia?
Tú no tuviste nunca la culpa de la lluvia.

Was it your fault that it rained?
No, the rain was not your fault.

—*Harold Lloyd, Estudiante*
Rafael Alberti
(translated by Mark Strand)

Well, good evenin',
don't that sun look good goin' down . . .

—*Milk Cow Blues*
Kokomo Arnold

Contents

one

two

three

one

1978–1982

Secret Warning

I made a mistake by not letting him in earlier, but as the day
was done I saw the ships in the desert and myself among them
and was then so prompted by memory I opened every door
    again,
although it seemed late. Sometimes when I walk now I find

the proportioned grasses anxious and bluer than usual, and
    they
stiffen fondly down side streets in the wind, and a few
    narrower
channels where there is life, and their preparation of memory
arrives in the box like a misshapen letter, ancient

and green in its refusal to reveal any formal message
we could understand to its end. I used to smell the past
in what felt like a tonal arrangement of bridges and the faces
under them, and the danger of drawing too close to them only

colored them more intimate than a stranger. Strangers and
their symbols of grief were among them, a few ill birds
flapped baldly until he departed, and hastened from one
    stairway
to the next. This going down did not end, and the house

was as token with its apparition as it was angry by offering
you a hand you could not take, because holding that hand
    would have
only led nowhere. It wouldn't have been nowhere, but
    beginning
again, getting out of the way, struggling with your own sense

of being victimized even as no one hung around to blame.
Was there anyone in the wind, was their hand as simple a thing
as memory, a river you wouldn't take, deciding instead
to believe in a small place for refuge. You even had trouble

beginning the fire, but didn't go on anyway. There were no
apparitions then, you sought them so directly it was like
two past friends meeting in the past with nothing so much
as even color to greet them as they staggered into the desert.

What was there in his face?, and in the crisp shadow the tower
formed, edging itself off in the briefest of winds so that the
shadow too was brief. You could have sworn you felt a few
    geese
dropping in the air behind you, but these were gone before

you even turned, and left you with the dark feeling of a
    message
but nothing finally therein. Just as if the letter had
some proposition to give you. I turn nervously away from you
only because you greet me the same, I make up stories

of having to check the box again and this makes me happy.
I go down the stairs again not to return. I spent the morning
reading about geese and death, and somehow feel
I will never be the same. There is a neighboring bridge

over a neighboring river where you could tell this story
again and again, and someone there would listen. Someone
would tell you the story is too dark because of its deadness.
The story would go on. Small ships or boats would bring

strangers you could sleep with, and someone would help them
    down
with your own memory, and bring them into the bald land.
You would reach out to them as never before, and would
    remember
nothing. You would be like them, just as they are.

As the river divided among you you could shift in your sleep,
taking only a few for refuge, but watching more closely
as the beginning hung in the sky and trees, the box
listening from its own life of messages, lit by the passing fire.

There would be nothing to say. The fog
creeps down the river. It would say *Look in.* The fog
would creep down the river. It would say *Look in.*
It would tell me to take its hand, *Look in.*

The Blossoms

are you nervous with me?
don't be.

blossoms are nervous,
men who lift their

tits to the sky are
nervous,—not me.

Love alters all nervousness
in the glory of said

nervousness:
I securely fasten my cap

to the door of my nervousness
and tell no one. The blossoms

still list with simple stones,
I give up my sense of voice

to the world and for this
was less, they told me so.

I gave my sense of day in
smallest conversation.

White Envelope on Black Sweater

I guess it will be possible
to keep pressing my head against
a small corner of the window, the most
awkward of the corners. To keep looking
for you and your visitation I have stayed here,
and pressed my deck of 52 cards closer to me
today, and for longer than usual. The cold waters
at the top of the stairs are lit by daylight,
I've had to turn down many invitations to walk up.
One night the unfinished business of the window
spoke to me about taking a job the next morning,
that was a surprise. But they didn't begin work
yet, so at least now I have some other time to adjust.
My childhood ghost has not walked here,
although the man at the top of stairs
said, no. I saw them yesterday. If I would
only go up.
Sometimes the unfinished business of children
is more complicated than our world, a contagion
of snow and white bells, just like that letter
I tossed on the bed today, so it may construct
its womanly village in the valleys of my sweater.
I just want to get that letter out of here.
If you hadn't arrived, I could've kept saying
all I needed today, as if the fall were late,
for once postponed, the valley park waving its few branches
a few green blocks down the street. I'm glad I never
walked out there. When I see that park I think of
her, and it's hard on me. Who would begin working
7 years ago on a deck of cards? I did.
I had left her then, and began taking out the deck
secretly to myself, I spoke so much to myself

it was all I could do. I saw waters in the face
of the queen, and the jack and the 4 traveled to
Bolivia just a few months ago. I haven't seen
them either. All I needed at this window today
was to see you, so I could see the lost season,
on time again, as it has been in the past.

In the Rain, in the Odd City

It seems I should have noticed the others,
the others burning in the forest boats,
and how unusual it is to be late
because of them.

The rain has fallen so long tonight
that now the square makes a false reflection—
it seems like there are carriages where
there are only people standing,

it seems like the hour
is a diploma of false rain,
that there is no memory,
that the streets continue with madness

until they end where the fields are,
where the backward water washes
against the back forest.
This is only the hope of a meditation.

That there is no memory—
that this is the graduate death
stepping out of his carriage
in the rain, in the odd city

in the middle of the forest.
The voices bend, a train's whistle
equally bends: if there is no memory
there is no accident. You may wonder

why I keep such odd hours,
why I never get reviewed. Rationale:

I have forgotten almost every name,
so the names return in the forest boats,

with horror I write each new name
in my ledger, and I am the horror
who is only a keeper of names.
Names, my friend, names.

Turn off your light
and say the word names, names.
Names, names.

Yesterday I followed the mad fireeaters,
who were fighting for the title of fire.
One of them awoke
and asked for her grades.

"Sometimes there was some image of a fire.
A few children surrounded their tub with lit candles
and the fire of the boat people emptied out
over no houses. In the hideous city of the forest
only small spaces of unlit sky
where the memory can return again."

The Shadows Are Ripe

I knew I had to start somewhere
so here I am with my postcard
of Matisse's THE MOROCCANS
for assurance and color although
many would tell you it's a poor
copy. But it's enough for me today
and it's free and even though you
can't see it believe me when I say
it's harder to figure out than most
guess; I personally believe and feel
there is a gas station pump in this
fragmented apartment of Matisse's
and obviously feel it is a fragmented
apartment in four or five parts and
how a pump got there is beyond me.
It is 1916 which is even more beyond.
Another one he did I have and even sent
some extras to friends; I forget the title
but one detail is an unhappy boy at his
piano lesson and part of his face is
like the hatchet I once had in mind and
put in a poem as a father's face many
years before I ever looked much at
Matisse. Which is maybe why it's a
favorite although forgetful in particulars
as favorites of mine are.

Someone said in a book that most desire
to eat can be solved by drinking water
or other non-harmful beverages. Today
when I was looking at my crooked teeth
in two mirrors to see how crooked they

look to everyone else I thought that
the statement by that someone is one of
the most ridiculous I have ever heard,
and wanted to forget it before following
it along.

The sun keeps dripping behind clouds and
light keeps changing. Betsy and Charlie
get back from their honeymoon today.
Five days. They were going to fish.
It's time to write my brother—the shadows
are ripe yet I don't know what to say.
I'm sure I hurt Bern by not stopping by
after the wedding.

I wonder if the earth will shake tonight.
Where will the tremors be? Wonder what
happened to the hatchet face I made for the father.
I couldn't ever tell if it was tender, cruel
or somewhere awful in between.

Directly in Shadow

Sometimes it gets lonely here,
the sea water collapses
out beyond the horizon
like the dream I thought
I understood, only to find
waking harder than the dream's horizon.

The vessels cast off
with their black cloth
—directly in shadow
the sails are strange,
stories of haunted spoons
rattling in the house wind.

Billy DeSantis, why
did I dream you? Like
bad writing you called me
'Chicken' in the dream.
I admonish you now,
100 umbrellas later.

Examine other faces from school:
their eyes feeding
crows, their mouths and ears
always home for the evening,
lonely as flames
or empty boats.

Nothing today is as
the dream was, the umbrella
is not entangled in a deck of cards,
the other umbrella did not, in 1923,

Passing into
and out of
the bed
mirror
cracked
dreams
shadows
stuck
to the
walls

We fought off
the
blackbirds
In cracked
leather
houses
we watched
to houses
wrinkle
and shrink

to shrinkle

13

write the story "Isaac Babel."
The editor did not return home.

House with only sails, spoons,
pasted faces, kiss me
on my left breast
with your one dollar stamp.
Kiss me with the horizon's current.
Tell me there is no face beyond the dream.

The Fellatio House

Walk with me now beyond the object of your desire,
past the unfortunate granite which has been given
this foolish position
I will effectively keep no company
I will effectively amble upon the local streets
with a semi-friend who does not in the least way
get along with another semi-friend, and they keep me
between their glares when they meet
I will effectively say, time is useless, I told you so,

I will effectively scribble my violent words as a rejected lover
upon the
hearsay lawyers build their fortunes upon,
I will effectively, and twice, injure them in my dreams.

There is no road like suicide,
I will effectively keep that in mind,
I will effectively keep a list of each contagion:
summer and smoke replaced by fire and smoke, no winter bells
for memory, no lamps darkening the snow with their shadow.
I will effectively adore Kim Novak because of her mistakes,
because of my mistakes
I will kiss your hose goodbye. Goodbye hose!
A crisis begs for a cigarette,
I will effectively smoke it /

Now then, now then,
sit down and discuss this effective uselessness
of god with me, raise the ante, call!
3 depravations!

3 Kim Novaks—one. A presley and a Novak.

e's Tongue

Dear Diane,
take me back.
I'm writing you, when I should be phoning
to order my telephone book of the present.
1953 was a year I also loved.
$2 + 16$ exacted praise for advancement,
and I was told to return home like a horse
drawing the wagon of the winter storms
of all unhappy children in Rome, New York.
I had permission to leave the table only after
answering whether there was life 'out there,'
after citing the brutal friendships of the future
which would crack like the vision of a man reading
a book in the mirror. After citing Susan
C's awkwardness when she was in motion,
her eye which was without leaves,
she who darkened like the consciousness of her awkwardness.

Prescience, I'm sure, these mutual journeys
to the tombs of our pasts.
The mirrors of the yellow addresses
help no one dress now, or shave,
or alter the sad ties no one wears (ever!).

Let us compare notes on the dancers:
John Adjournment waltzes with Anguished Storm
(he hasn't shaved since 1953, her dress
is only feverishly buttoned),
William the Listener wants to kiss Mental Illness,
but she is coy, and he accepts this.
Stupid Idyll stands in the gymnasium corner

with his gang, the Local Discomforts.
They're going to make a fool of Roger Judgment
before the night is through. Everyone will be
pleased, except for William the Listener,
who might even consider counter-action,
but will probably only say 'Doesn't anyone here
have feelings,' and walk away (he said the same thing
in 1963, when the White Victories laughed as he cried
after a first viewing of West Side Story. But then
that story was full of whites, and flickered out with
a fake white voice). John Uriarte dances quietly
and late, and was given a tie for the occasion.
But he is the butt of our jokes also, because
we are so surprised.

But what I have waited to tell you with longing
is the walk home of one Jimmy O'Connor,
poor and helpless in the gym
but now briefly alone under the shovel of stars
as he removes his sad shoes and the contrived tie
he wore for hours and is making fun of death
and any career. I know only what he told me
one Saturday morning as I delivered a paper
to his flat. He was sweeping the floor
and said I don't want any career. Not me.
He said it out of the blue. Out of the same blue
I asked how old he was. 'Eight. Any objections?'

Many years later, this summer, I was sitting
with Irma who was telling me of her friend
'She grew up and spent her childhood in France . . .

I think of the confused feelings of all loves,
a woman from Belgium and a woman from France.
I hear a solemn fool telling me I have no feelings.
I consider this so.

Let love's tongue deliver the past from us,
be well.

Where did Jimmy hear the word career?
Why do I have no feeling?

And where are you, Thomas Burch,
who as my friend loved every girl
I ever loved, and asked if you could dance with them and did,
and took them home.

And Anthony Pinti, whose voice I imitated one Saturday
when I called my girlfriend Pat, and she, with all feeling,
believed it was him. Anthony honey why haven't you called.

There is a cheap berry of a moon rising,
I have no feeling for this blanche moon.
Blanche! Now there is a name. Did you see what Blanche
    wore . . .?

Untitled

Think to yourself
the most circular
path, the green
book by

the green river,
and how night
calls softly
one there,

as if you are
water, or a
message before
it is given,

like the word
by the river,
by the word
next to it

Four in a Field

Here is the table
and the photograph of
a beautiful woman
reading in her light

and when there was a time
where the field
was black with pheasants
before the river

closed out and
the jobs taken like
a hat soiled
from disuse

or four in a field
the mother and father
and child
and a friend of theirs

and the four deer
come upon in
the night under
the autumn moon

who is to say which
luck was given
by whom to each
deer

and who is to
say that this didn't
happen that it isn't
so

Stoney Lonesome

Stoney lonesome. Gnaw-
bone. A house
sits back from
the road.
                 —*Robert Creeley*

Want to see
Pricey's father,
unseen in 12
years, and their
house there in
the dark as I've
seen it so long

Want to think
it still possible
to marry Mary Ann
as my sister said
Mary Ann had wanted
one week when we
were ten.

Want to know if
there's a song for
Pricey's grave his
friends left on,
or even better
a song for his life
to pass upon,
hand on.

⌣⌐

Could you bring me
news of your new love,
how you waited in the flat light,
listened for him?

Here is the melted coin
kept for you, weak
with an incorrect story
of another dark hole,

this one hidden back
in the woods
where we followed.

Here is the stoney lonesome thief,
house from the hill,
hard
to keep the life going.

w from Breathing

I will take my pulse
when "father"
is in

the shop,
I will tap
my fingers

on the table
tops—shadow from
a mirror,

shadow from breathing.
I will hear his
forgiveness,

I will place it
like a hatchet
in a bowl of

amnesia
a bowl of loud rain
which parts

everything
in half. I will
I will

return this
love book
so signed by

its author
and I will
meet the rent

with an axe,
not unlike
Raskalnikov

or his maker
who is responsible
for this

way of thinning.
Because it was a
way of thinking

I spent the longest
time pretending
it was true

which it isn't,
and what attributes
I could give

this "father."
He is not mine,
he is postponed

from younger
years, which I
divided by task

from other summers.
Loved one, you
are at school,

the bells are
ringing, the yards
fall off into

fear.

One Day

one day of paper
one day of rain

and I've wanted
to read his

letters again, or
stall within them
from their underground

passages of blinding
color and muted
stillness—which

there is no other
word for

although a muted
steamy white
falls from

the left love.

It is all love:
a box-like
clock upon the
mud road, the wren's

neck
still
from suffering.

Stilled
is the approach
to the paper

and to the rain
or from the
stalls of
yellow hay,

as simple a thing as
alleged ends
are.

When the Sun Rises

I do not know how I need the air,
or if it needs me. The lost air,
the air which is smashed, like a red hat.
When the sun rises the amnesty
of the unused animals—the goat, the burrow,
the maroon horses—when the sun rises
the amnesty of these flies its flag: an orchard
with a thumb on top.

I called the artist "beyond the rain"—this
was the name I called rent, landlord, sorry
angry name, angry name like a drowned finch.
A finch which was hanged. A finch which cried.

Who cries like the trees? When my soul dreamt
it would be beside me I made a mistake in asking
for its sex, an act of violence dominated the doubleness
of the dream, like there was sand where there was once just
    gravel
and no road, only a lonely dream of road.
A derrick in another city is the same road, the red and yellow
colors mean it.

The island was red. I could wash the artist
and the island was red. It was an afternoon
when bombs fell from the sky like dead birds,
like dead clouds, clouds of tomorrow, skies of fame
for the dead artist. The dead world.

I want my sister to call me into this field
of crying trees. I want her slow bells, tolling
far across the roads which hang back among trees
from the other road. The main road is always other,
what other name could it be?

Far Sight

I went to sleep
with my invisible,
and stories of
grief and blue lights

gleamed with some
profound height,
and a green bag
rode high with

the wind, and the
voice closed. Where
will the wedding
be, what friend will

turn leaf by leaf
trying to hide
me? If there is
a place to stand

is it daylight,
the shore which
is gaudy with
separateness, doubles

of word and other
inventions of the
sky, like the sea
at the sky, the day

fell. I ride to the
end of a private
place and the rock

fell from fear,
the punishment of
wishing for my own
turned upon each

image which burned,
the river and the past
which burns in it,
hands too. Images

like small women
and small men,
I don't know. If
a woman touches

blue light from the
mountain I hear
a heartbeat, if
a man concentrates

I see a glass kite.
The buildings have
their windows open,

forgetfulness leans out
in the stairway of
a white figure, and
the ghost returns to me

long enough to turn
the door, and the lights
go out. A star reports
to another star.

Mood Indigo

This is a letter to no one,
who is twenty years old,
who is a fifteen year old necktie,
the sky, alone in the world.
Sky: you are a family of aloneness now.

Four, five, six
and you must return the violets,
which mate with the lonely wind.
Tents flap beside them, and request
the sudden loneliness of death.
Seven memories: a broken windowpane,
a boy shifting in sleep, a shoe
worn on the second finger of the right hand.

And there is a disease
the letter refers to as skin,
indigo skin. An afternoon which
was lonely for the night. Oh night,
oh night so forgetful, fragment of rain,
maybe the night is rain.

Maybe you are no one, like the night.
Like why are you thinking of a pilot
whose star is crossed, a pilot light which burns and burns,
a pilot alive with motherhood.

The mood is a train, the shoes are watches.
The man with clocks boards the train and evaporates.
The tent is a deep breath, underwater.
You are a slave to shaken reason.

My umbrella stared at the sky as the conversation died,
and outside I saw my friend drive off for one last night
of listening to white's voice, yellow's voice.
I made a choice which involved paradise but paradise
burned up, and the houses put violets out.
I went back to my grandfather, he who was buried like a
    candle.
The stones were second names, names of birds,
birds which suddenly cry for you, but you are asleep.
What you hear is the early wind, wind from a hand,
a face. You can't decide what to do, whether you are wounded,
whether you are locked out. Who is the loyal rain,
where are you?

A Small Closed Room

There are pictures so old, my little Alma,
I don't know why I keep them anymore,
they have no record for me. It might be
a falseness, or a problem of our privacy,
why we didn't live in the real world,
as if there was one, but there must have been
someone there because we kept saying to ourselves
it was real, the world, or someone. I told you
one day, as you were going to model, I would only be
the happiness before your truest happiness, and there
you would spend your life, and you laughed at me.

I don't know why I keep these records anymore.
I don't know why
it's a problem of privacy. I guess
I stopped when we stopped, someone
who was not the world, whoever that was.
Which one comes early with the early light
of evening, which is the last early light,
and on any day how do you live on? It is too bright
for me here, and the birds sing, I don't know their names
and don't want to, it is enough that they sing, I look
out a small closed room I put myself in and look out at them
sing, I can't breathe when I do that.

Evening is the one residue of light I can't stand.
Actually, a few hours before this I can't stand it.
I despise it. I despise what I easily said
to supposed friends. It's all my own doing,
then they listened. Then they said it back.
I hate that backness as I hate the summer evening

for giving backness to light. Last light,
my eye.

I will never see you again, I said that.
I will die.

Gin. White Out.

Sometimes there are too many exclamations in the world, and
   they're all pulling out.
Stopping short of blue, white, stopping short of the bay
   window. There's no bay
on the other side of this bay window, but you can sleep there,
   on this side of it,
even holding the hand of the tree, on this side of it, if you care
   to. I'm here,
like a diary who was told by his parents, "grief is the best
   thing, so don't you
believe them." I believe them, keep searching for them,
   whoever this them is.
I used to think it was the window, *them* was the windows, so
   often I talked to them.
I'd even ask you here now, there are a lot of windows. But there
   isn't much else.
Their mere desire for the crystal to hang there, at the bay, on
   the other side,
keeps me here. But the crystal too is pulling out on me,
the social worker gives me a lot of shit, and the hand of the
   tree
happened once to take someone else into it, took the pitiful
   shit and abruptness
down into it, like they take the darkies down, hoping to see
   both the mother and the boy
or the father and daughter both rising, their chops off,
somewhere now inside their

hands. I drive by it, whether it is the usual truth, I drive by this
   house.
Individually, the crystals separate catastrophe into light—not
   song

but light. Light does this. When light does this there can't be
    song.
And whether this is the usual truth the house and the crystals
    walk
through the diary: they deny song, as they should, as so much
    which is used to them.
Nothing migrates, especially song. Once I worked in a hospital.
One of the doctors wanted to lock you up. Someone talked him
    down.
I didn't say much. I knew and didn't know. Someone did know,
    so they talked.
I'm arrogant shit even to mention this. It fills in nothing, the
    fact of it,
like the fact of yours, pulling out. Whitening out used to take
    place
in the eyes. Again, they weren't my eyes, but I heard of it.
    When the white
became blue, you saw this. You said: a sleeve walks into a
    parlor. The sleeve
sits down and begins to deal cards. I'm asked to leave the room.
    I go for
a brief drive. By the time I return the sleeve is giving me a lot
    of shit—
where are your crystals, we can't land without them, and if you
    pull out on us
we're going to burn you out, we're going to separate you, the
    white from the blue,
which isn't so bad, except we'll deal you out, we'll deal you
    into song.

Eating on a Starlit Porch

The man with clocks
is my amnesia,
is a hatchet in
a bowl of milk,
is my happiness
on a cool evening
under a new moon,
is a sentence
eating on a starlit porch,
is a fact of lunacy,
years and years,
is the schoolyard

where her shoes sleep,
is her off-white robe
which she closed
for the last time,
seven times, on
a long summer
morning, is your
sleep which is a
man with clocks, is,
is years and years,
is my rent, my
journal, my
never, my return.

Woman on a Train (Le Mistral)

An obsessive figure without any
horizon to her. A shadow and a bell.
A river without a song. The mind
in its incomplete arc.

The woman who was hanged
has been dropped out, the woman
witness drops behind the garden,
the space created for the dead woman

loses clothing, loses love, loses,
loses. It was the mind which did this,
the passive mind, an obsession
for holes. The mind is a river

with a hole for a song, or without
a hole it is a song anyway, but it
is not the river. The arc is the
river's rope which is beside

the woman, passive and more
passive. A bell sounds out over
the town at least hours later,
and the bell is more for the mind

than the woman. The horizon
is a bell, a bell taking bags
to a cart, and the tongue leans over
with obsessive exhaustion.

The bell is a river of horizons,
with obsessions and holes. The mind

is only a figure at the window.
You cannot see the woman from the window,

so this says a lot about the mind.
What can the mind see? Trees,
stark tree, poplars and maples
up against the dark. Parts

of the river have no tree,
other arcs have many. But the river
has no windows, only its clear
obsessive figure looking back,

looking on. The exhaustion is
loss, the mind is loss. The mind
is loss. It loses the river
at the arc. The garden is a tired

hung theme, not even interesting
as a proverb anymore. It witnesses
back the mind at the window.
The mind at the river witnesses.

When will the hole in the bell
toll, and for whom will it be?
For the horizon is a bell
upon the river, towing

its obsessive hole. Towing
its own. It is always its own,
which is so much like the mind
the river is complicate,

so the mind sees that way.
The mind sees loss, any more
loss and the mind will flow
crazily, it will go crazy.

As they say the song is like
this so they also say I have
discovered a cart to take
my song home in, and its

hung theme caresses the
river when. When the river
when arcs the woman on the train
is dead, the mind is dead,

so be it. The song is a bell
for when's obsession, whatever
that may be, and where.
Carry it within, clothing.

9 / 5 / 81

feeling nothing as that
which is given
how slow I was to enter
anything within this green
boat—I must have waited
til I believed apprehension
had passed, as if it could, detaining
the dream from the end. There
was an end, for the end I
was sure. I ate the potato,
I went down into the shattered
hotel and ate another potato.
I held "your" breath—it wasn't
mine. My teacher sang from
a newspaper. My mother appeared
and demanded I start again—
I detained.

Yellow Evening

As the end was
some other way,
gazing from the window
onto otherness, the streets
like glass in the rain,
also clouds held
above by a stairway
of yellow evening,
light from other places.
When I was a cloud
the evening beckoned,
to prevent life I
turned from life, inside
where memory doesn't
so much distrust the fear
as it sharpens it:
a waterfall of endless
propriety, voices broken,
pitiful hole where a town
was, with places left on
for me.

My Sister Is Not a Dollar

I think it is unusual
I even try speaking, I hear steps and doors
where there is nothing but a medicinal smell,
the person crossing near me crosses on.

At the far end of a country lane
the night burned like shores,
the moon was dead, the moon
was okay.

The peace be and the peace
falleth, the garden is white
with my sister, and one dollar.

My sister is not a dollar,
I am not a man.

Not before the task,
when the burning afternoon rises
across the sky, not before
the angry residue of possession,
not before my teeth bleed
with greed for water . . .

not before. Here is the parting of nails,
frames, the parting of empty footsteps.

For Him

I will give you a
wall with my weight,
I will give you
a cemetery, an insolent
one, like the grey shovel
which is only tonight
the moon in the sky,
the clear memory of
your house, your death,
your goodbye to some
reason, which is rain's
forgetfulness.

Somewhere else, probably
just over the high place,
the high place of
each twilight, each
stain, somewhere over
there I say goodbye
to your sadness,
to your sighs from
personality: o hold me
fast and say I do
love the shadow of
clear sleep, the ruthless
disappearance of the hills.

Say to me you've forgotten
that no one
is love, no stream
is equal to another
stream except for

their white weight,
their shadows dropped
from the bridge of your
memory.

I hold you with no
money, the moment
ends and stays.
The days die
under the lamp
of a clear goodbye,
the evening disappears
with my family.

MR HOOK

mr hook died, i sought
refuge from women in
other women. i thought
of my father and i
thought of alcohol,

i did not know whether
this was my father thinking
or alcohol thinking, but i knew
it was not his alcohol,
it was mine, my thought.

poem against domination

thinking today of the endless character
of love, how the heart doesn't open,
how the walk back along the endless red gate
opens the cold sky, the trees flapping
like torn sleeves, the distant forest
some enactment, some . . . —song, the story
of existence, hers an industrious lax
silence given from another place,
another time, the door partly existence
and partly a door to cross. The mountain
the plan of this one endless accident:
so endless is the word for the morning sun,
for the hill the accident departed from,
cold as a knife and just as sharp,
the morning grey and green in minor shadows.

Candle of the Poor

I am so dead
I listen to the cars incorrectly,
and the wooden steam
is afraid you'll telephone
like a tear,
which is what I remember best
about being so dead.
And the lamp is a very distant voice
which is incorrect,
and the beginning of my childhood,
constantly suffered,
saying things twice.
I can still say something twice,
I don't know,
another careful wish
which like the candle of the poor
explodes. One reason it doesn't explode
is because I am so dead.
Incorrect, but dead.

Little Final Sunlight

station in Dover
Delaware, mint
green house,
facing it, the white
shade bending in
the little final sunlight
left. Light within
above clock,

people, even a head
or two. Or here
and there, out of time.

two

1982–1985

A Stranger Leaves Me

It is below, where she lives with a ruthless animal
named green, so named as green is both healing and sickness.
So why ruthless as the sound of a league, down there
where the green water beats the underside of the useless skin,

and down there where the house still cries out her name,
the incarnation of the other name, and the other names
are not names of the lost but—but brown and black and yellow

glasses, washing the chest of the child, washing
the eternal mind. Tell me: if I open my eyes will they be
    colorless,
will you go away with a key, walk with a candle, close the door
with a key: it was she below the door, a very intense cough,
a liquid night: because, perhaps, because the key always

turned in water. My sound today: as a result of my sadness
I am no longer sad. I see the boats, I see the rope, the other
    lamp
is extinguished by a past tense: a cloud passes above the boats
and a stranger leaves me. So much for the stranger who
    worshipped

these three boats out there on the plain, calm, blue horizon
as the bay is these things today, and the names of these clouds
above them are a mess: names which are a mess, forgetting
the mess of these lost messed names, which I maimed,

which I am poor for their loss, my forgetting.
I was so insane they are glad for my forgetting. If I take
a name like John, or Samuel, or plain Elizabeth . . .
if I am green as the names' other side.

I can't stop writing you. You, the pleasure which exiled me for
    awhile.
You of the whom dream, the bell swinging with echoes of two
    or three
notes as if from another bird, before the major echoes from the
    same
voice. I did not intentionally walk shores of light. I said my
    heart
is sick because it is not full. But . . .

I Entered a House

I have this tremendous fear of dying, tomorrow,
whether I stay or go. I have this tremendous
fear of suffering in death, whether I shave or
don't shave, whether I kiss you, or you kiss me,
or no one kisses anyone for the time being.

I have this tremendous fear I entered a house
which forgot about me, and still forgets,
and the clocks are still suffering, waiting
for someone, anyone, to cross their legs, to
light a cigarette, to leave.

While, while. Anyone leaves. I had a dream
and now I can't find it. I am sleeping in a kiss,
my clothes are sleeping. It was still
raining, I was
walking out of my shoes.

North and South

It is a strange couch, a couch
I cannot remember until I forget:
two doorways, north and south, two doorways
swaying in brown, yellow and black wind.

I have nothing to say.
A lamp explodes in my grandmother's grave.
Open your heartbeat. Fatal jealousies
called us upon the couch: the pilot,
the thin evening steps of the pilot.
He took up more space than my grandmother
and there were four of us on the couch.

And the winds from your family!
Your mother, your father who had such an intense heartbeat
the sun dried us when he sat there,
though he stood, still abusing you
in the forgotten ear of your fear.
And I stood still.

Scattered coins and clothing on the couch,
to make it look as though I'd fallen,
then taken another fall, and another.
Your telephone, always unplugged.
Did we need your telephone? We thought so.
We needed:

minds, minds, minds. They guided us,
people selling books in the useful shops of the mind.
And the moon shared my trousers, and the sun
shared your blouse, and we disrobed so very slowly.

Your mother had brown hair.
Your sister had brown hair.

It was in these silences our hearts broke,
in the never attended.

I have a very high fever, a bad one.
I can give you this but I'd rather not.

It's okay. It is a strange couch,
north and south, two doorways . . .

There Is No Night

Because they came from
their holes, I fed them.
I was a postal person
feeding twenty cats. Each
morning. Is it night in
the tunnel,—no, this is
because it is a children's
story, and in these stories
there is no night. There
are cats to feed in
the morning, but no
nights. Not in the tunnel,
not elsewhere. Two workers
while working told me
children want fear, so
my story wouldn't work,
—I thought of fear,
felt it days before but
not since, couldn't add
fear. I was simply
a postal clerk feeding
twenty cats every morning
on Water Street. They
came and they went,
I fed them. They expect
me. They may expect
fear during the day, I
don't know. I know there
are no nights, not in
the tunnel, not in the lot,
I know there is fear, but
not in this story unless

fear is a feeding of
one to one to one, washing
its face, deepening breath
the washing of one to one
to one. Not twenty,
but one. That is fear.

sia

There is no amnesia
like my amnesia,
based upon yesterday
and forgetfulness
just as I was told.

Told also by starry night:
I've forgotten the permanent kiss
which reared its breath
across today or tomorrow,
whichever day was present

in the starry darkness. Today,
tomorrow, who cares?
Only to caress my amnesia,
to take thy name inside me.
What was your name,

who are you?

The Sick One

the key to her story
seemed fear, as the
various incidents
unfolded the single
constant was spying,
like the old woman
watching her and her
husband years back,
climbing the hill
nearby in the old
car, and then for
no known reason even
writing later, writing
I saw you—

old given: those who spy and
spend their time being watched
are bound to develop phobia
of leaving house, rooms, self:
at least this unfolds with her
version. The forest for the trees.
and the suffering seems mild,
and the comic aspect wild as well
as mild, it seems like a point to
say this was not such a bad way
not if now the leaving could
bring relief. of the 7 or 8
variously described the one
most various: the marriage collapses,

and years later the husband
still furious as she chose not

to carry that excess weight
of *his* name, and him now up on
the hill too, though happily
remarried, sitting with spyglasses
with the old woman, watching
the so-called ex return to that
spot. Somehow the sister had
even gotten in on this, passed
it on to the old lady, who knew
the man, and they sat up on the
hill watching the sick one.
She returns.

A Study in Scarlet

nothing to see in that horror
except a truer version of the other,
echo of island, unfaithful father
to the point of abuse, and then the
romantic abuse, the same life lived
again. not much more to say than
to see. she rides in a car beside
him, rides and rides. some dogs bark,
the shit hits the fan. that and lust
and a few conversations, the bodies
joined in the holy terror of the thing,
not knowing, the bones knowing
but drifting out there off the island—
and it isn't the calm image it seemed
to intend, more a bobbing and shaking,
more a don't go, don't do this. and then
they went again anyway and the bones
got awfully tired, so much so the mind
even began to follow and despite resistance
its breath died down some. A Study in Scarlet
was always a favorite theme, almost as if

a painting from the old
comic cover, the *rach*—the name
half ended, half begun. a discreet
red life sitting in the back of
the mind like an object, like
the mental picture of a harbor
with her there, a reminder of
lament and smoke, the constant
saying something, the constant
father teaching. No wonder he chose

to remember as much of it as he can,
just to look—it was that gazing
which embedded the painting from
the old red room, the painting of
the theme years before it ended.
No wonder one believes in the abstract
as the pure, the garbage of the theme,
the life left endlessly in abuse.
She can want it or not. I always
thought the abstraction was a theme,
something to touch, knew *that*
was there, the tactile sense of it.
But didn't know this til today,
looking into the cadence of the
horror, the counterpart of my
denial. Like the recovered drunk

yelling you can't do this and then
the key to the cell just clicking,
and at 4 a.m. officer officer in a low
murmured voice, what did i do?
The pang there. Be true not with
the moon, for that may be a dead thing,
there for the living to see—I don't
know. It was a thought one morning,
having to take the dog there, and seeing
it up there, over south of the cemetery.
A reminder. With the morning star
far to the east. Then it was a few
days later, passing the tomb, he
died in 1953, the wife recently
interred, and upon his the heaviness

of Soldier & Judge. One would
get the point across. Who needs
it? But for the solution of that
memory I do not recall, nor is the
need there, in that place. It goes
as all love, unavoidable. There is
a story of the wind dropping into
a forest of trees by water, the plain
man and the plain woman, their heads
almost birdlike, and the story doesn't
end with a moon or a star or even
memory. It just ends.

Strangely Insane

I could not eat much
as a child.
Now I eat and I have debts.
No child acquires debts like mine
and I find this unfortunate.
For if my debts were a child
I could pay in rain,
I could pay in repetition
I could pout like a garbage can
between two garages.
I could sell berries, cheaply,
to my dead neighbors.
I could make them undead.
I could make half the city sun,
half the city fog, so everyone (there)
could sigh, except for some unfortunates
upon whom my visitations would most
selfishly beat. And they could
drive me away to stars in apogee,
to corner stores, to market places
where death is an eerie island.

I am waiting for your portrait.
That will please me. That will please
the ghost I presumptuously ate for you.
Help me. Hold me. I am inside a light
I cannot recall. Skyless.
Strangely, as they say, insane.

In here it reads: orange leaf,
misunderstanding the ways we were lost,

there is no we which trembles.
It reads and reads . . .

I could not eat much as a child.
Go away, go away, go away.

I Can Tell You I Was Very Sad to Receive Your Piece of Sentiment

I can tell you it was too loud.
I can tell you when I heard the door close
on the street at night, can tell you were there,
miles away, with a dog guarding the doors
of your house, with a lost sister guarding
your window, with a lost mirror of someone
like myself reflecting all the ugliness he could muster.

I can tell you there are moments
when a grave opens its face
in a book upon the shelf,
whether the book is opened or not—
that the face is already forgotten,
has an odd brush for eyebrows,
combs for teeth, very small combs.
My sister brought me this book
while I was still young, young crescent moon
without any name yet, without any full face,
tired (so young to be so tired) of lacking
these things but still, yes, rising.

Can tell you my father intentionally
broke your eyeglasses
so you would not depart, so I would not
depart soon after, tell you I understood
his inquiry with himself before he even began
and so headed him off at the pass
of the evening twilight, the grandeur
at the pass of the lovely blue corridors
where he began his first childhood
and so resorted upon that evening
to childish behavior, breaking eyeglasses.

I can tell you my spiritual advisor—
the road upon the night, the road
upon the day, the person beside me
who talks and I listen—can tell you
he said life has begun to be déjà vu—

oh candlelight upon your face,
oh sad shadow of screen across your breast,
oh love of life in my shadow—
these, and the winter nights beside you,
I remember and forget.

⌒

I'm still haunted by the story,
the imposter's life, the living
in the hotel under an alias.
What a strange phrase—under an alias,
the name assumed! The alias
assumes wicked proportions, even a weird sense
their lives had become parallel
and met. Upon that night

I called to you in death—
it wasn't sad, it wasn't death,
I wasn't certainly
either marginal: sadness or death
but it was that feeling,
the boney one, one from the heart,
which wakes the brain.
The brain loves to sleep on nights like this,
divide the body.

Your body and mine—now there were two bodies.
I love you beyond any palpable belief—
beneath the door where the sea wakes,
beneath the sea, old candlelight.

Nothing is awful without you.
As for the imposter: I can tell you
my breaking heart breaks hearing
his tall tale, or for the real one,
but that is not the truth,
nor is the truth grief or fear.
It is better sometimes to talk
of the past as truly abstract,
that in that way of telling the tale
one might still rendezvous,
create a belated appointment.
Better to change the names and the adjectives.

Today there is no Lisa or Paul,
today there is no happily or insane.

Words are such prisons,
I am always looking for the door.

Where is my key,
where is the dream of my friend
who tells me to not give away so much,
where is my alcoholic memory,
is it dead?

What can I do when I call the night
stupid, want to spend the rest of my life
feeding you? It was a vast mistake
to tell you nothing, and now someone other
tells you everything.

The city could not perfect us,
nor the fields.
We lived in the jails
and in the sea.

We were a single horse, public and alone.
We were struck by a pair of shoes,
which belonged to no one special,
as the lifelong seriousness belonged
to no one special, no one ridiculous
either.

The idiot speaks because the shadow
undresses him. And then his voice
is hers. He has no voice. It is her voice.

Sea and Pine and Storm

I never looked into the small box—
could have been weather, sea and pine and storm,
could have been failure, that kind of longing—
either of these various conditions kept me away from the box
and very awake.

Fictions from the Self

I am in a hurry to decide two things: whether my
amnesia has any color to it, whether the ghastly
charity of hope is nothing more than that adjective
I've chosen: ghastly.

Because: my amnesia seems to have a desire to repeat
itself, and in that form of repetition is not destined
to be different than my prior lack of amnesia. In
this case the amnesia may not even be mine, more or
less some prolonged pattern, and in this case would
have a color, something like magenta, some color perhaps
slightly cooler than that.

I can remember the magenta portrait in the cool hallway
of my aunt's farmhouse, an old lady—the portrait—
probably of victorian times. The dark frame, so like
the wooden banister of the stairwell. Passing it at
night. Never fond of this thing for itself—if anything
it gave me the creeps—but the passing itself becoming
an act of location, an act of devotion, regardless of
even any terror the portrait might bring to reign.

Which brings me to the ghastliness of hope: which for
some like myself used to abide in memory, or in amulets,
or in the faces of others, arms of others, tales of their
past and future others brought to me, and I listened.
But hope was a wish somehow strangely avoiding any abiding
in the present—at bay out there, true abeyance, adrift,
off the coast. I can feel the current of desire to go
to that place as just such a ghastly hope.

And the ghosts there—of course. The fictions from the
self:

self which married, self which married houses, steeples,
light from the bay sky on the back road . . . the evening
grasses, the figures there, each in some still motion as
I passed, always passing . . .

Like a Receipt

Went walking with a few others
in the guarded sunlight of hilly
streets, saw a man through the door,
beyond another man, assumed owner,
bequeathed to the street for only
a moment: saw the fat man sitting
there in black, like a receipt,
a fat black receipt waiting and waiting:
o deliver love and no other word,
deliver flawless feeling to the house,
the feeling that comes once in a lifetime,
then, when least looking, once again.

Story of Marie

There were many sounds I was raised with—
hammers, coughs, exhaust—exhaust creates
a hiss in the brain following morning coughs,
the cars close by the window, father coughing,
mother sneezing, brother playing hammer with a fist . . .

—and then there were the sounds of Marie,
slow tablets I listened to as the morning progressed,
tablets of song and smoke, smoke I felt in the back of my brain
behind the hiss, the song I felt beneath her heart . . . heart
which was a city, city of forged letters, forged secrets:

secret passages to my secret sister, my secret brother . . .
phantoms which hovered and dropped over the glasses my
      mother wore.

And there was the stillness
after the sound, not unlike the story
my uncle told me, the head beheaded, the head
lolling and trembling off. The depths
of such a story interfered with an otherwise

contented life. These depths were plumbed also:
by Marie, so named by her family
for the pheasants which fell from the sky
on the day of her birth
pheasants which pursued her childhood:

there, in the shoes she wore,
in the braids in her hair:
pheasants, braille pheasants, which recited
the songs before they were sung by her attuned blind voice.

It seems now there is a singular condition behind the life,
mine and hers. It separates one from another like a bridge
separates a side of the river from the other side,
and the river is of course always flowing, starlit
under bridge.

And the singular condition drives one into the other:
stars driven into the river, shoes driven into songs,
life driven into another life. If the sounds are not dead
then they must be living,

and Marie's sober ghost locks up the white afternoon
upon the bridge, her father is almost home when he reaches
the bridge's midpoint: the relics hear him stopping, looking
    over,
and the pins and buttons and stuffed pheasants fall from the
    shelf . . .

here is Marie at work, so put off by her death her ghost is sober,
white like a false eye, an eye which never divides its gaze
and thus continually welcomes the pheasants back, and the
    braille
bridge, the braille water, the pounding of the braille upon the
    bridge.

Who can say my brother killed her,
who can say she killed my uncle,
who in their longing can say?

Within the stillness there is a cough, cough
from a white car passing by. I see her hand
murmur at the window, heading off

over the singular condition of what must be
an afterlife. There is no other reason

for the smoke, for the song which went:
one day my uncle took my head in his hands
and took it off, one day I heard a car sing.
Give me the ring from your finger,
give me the pheasant which sleeps in your bed . . .

the song is that condition,
like the condition of my brother,
my brother the tailor, forging the pheasant life,
never expecting my visit . . .

and I walk in as singular as the bridge I think,
and then the past coughs,
and Marie sings a song for my dead uncle.

Inside a Clock

I spent my life inside a clock,
yes. I took my manhood inside
a clock. Yes, I poured and poured

inside my clock. The building
creaks inside a clock: numb,
numb, numb. Like overseas

while one stands upon the shore,
overseas where the candle blows
indifferently and then, at night,

blows out
but lights again: or so one thinks
like night thinks. I thought.

I thought the goats herded by the sea,
as in the painting of the clock:
and the young, timid herder blew

into the wind with her voice—
overseas the snow walks, overseas
the melancholy sit among the stones,

among tables of potatoes, green
and numb and bladed where the sea
breaks out, like a man on fire

inside a clock. The wind blows
out but lights the houses and the sea
itself: the waves carry one back

on the waves, as in the wake of
the boat the waves clock, the clock
waves like night thinks, the fire

herds the goats. And there is that
clock there with the woman and the
snow. And the waves break young, timid,

The Hour Hand

Try not to test the iris
by saying: I will now place you

in the portal of reality, iris,
and so placed you shall forever
want. The iris

won't reveal
much of anything except
a stillness
in your so-called

real place. The high road
is white under the white sun

and even now under the white moon
the high road is still
white—the road

is also aflame with iris.
If I place the road I shall want
the road, the wanting

won't cease. When I worshipped
the dream—him always upon
the road, the hour hand
cheaply
beside him, cheap symbol of a dream—

when I worshipped him in this
dream I was always separated
from him, distances
revealed distances,—I remember,—another

true dream sign—I remember passing
a schoolhouse, an old one, a woman
there slowly moving across
a flame—I was in town to see
my aunt, but she died in the dream
before the second day
passed, I hadn't seen her—

only the sign of this woman,
schoolhouse and plight

of woman in that flame
vanished—the plight
easily mine.

In a night of flame
the eye's iris
still finds

a road—red flower,
unseen silence
within entire flames.

The morning was antiquity—
resetting the clock,
resetting the clock the love
in the painting

appeared smaller,
the painting smaller,
his love of himself

smaller, more defined.
An iris or two shone
in the carlight

which now seemed damp.
Oh for that dream
to clarify—

Picture with No Past to It

I followed the love story
pretty quickly. I had this thing
for my mother, I lost weight
by the shore, I held the feces

in my hand standing at the window
by twilight, watching the flowers to the far side
from the corner of my eye and my vandalism,
overlooking the orchard

and the abomidible faces which used the word
closely in a strange encounter of one course
with another course, the ships steering swiftly
upon the shattered voyage

of their own dreams, the ones they grew up with
and so absolved. When I stand in the love story
I grow up too, the flags which were torn asunder with the years
feel like Hollywood, and my mother

has taken a fireside hill on Mulholland Drive,
the light is dark as pie, the moon is a ridge,
and we smile like a bonfire as the abuse burns again
and the drive is in a twilight which understands, erases

mile after mile of fire. I have been
to the sea and I have been
back. I am no longer afraid
of my mother.

Mysteries

I don't know if the pain
would go away,
but if it would.

I don't know why the name rhymes,
there in the foggy field,

there beside the barn
across the treeless creek,

there where she made
her very first stroke,
and the mark took its place

for years and years.
I don't know if the pain
starts only when I think of it,

when I see her bending
and sliding in the name,

in the quarrel with hatred,
whatever it means.

I remember one night
asking how many mysteries
there were, how each, if each,

was cloaked in a silence
like the silence of a soul,
if souls are silent.

I remember hearing her voice
like a lonely thing sounds.

The Song Is Passing like a Wave

Many of the images refuse to part,
dictions of light still make up the light,
the broken theories depart like the water,
though the water did not depart: it is just waiting,

sounding, turning. Maybe I am still deluding myself,
like tearing up the pockets, crossing the white night
with an endless face in front of me, a signpost from warning,
and the list I would like to make of life,

the blue and the green and the yellow,
the illusion I could cite as the image,
memory as all my own disillusion, the song's refrain,
the song's shovel, the needing

of the arm and the body beside me,
the having you here, the management of the life:
seems that life came between the life,
at the ledge, at the window,

at that single saying of the candle in the red night.
Today I heard voices within the shovel,
voices of chain, voices of listening. The light
listed the sea as a separate voice,

I could tell my part in the desert with any kind clarity,
except that the desert held a sigh, held
it long, and I waited in red night
for your return. I waited in fear. I was embarassed,

for I recalled how I had not gone there for years and years,
how I had stopped where the water stopped, at the end,

at the edge where the beginning and the end
and my sight was a feeling for the call.

Years pass. I don't solve
anything. Someone breaks the images and they
break again, I hear the identity of the song.
The song is passing like a wave.

My Little Black View

When I pull the paper
against the metal it sounds as if
the telephone rings. I hear the tonal
warning for the ships, I see the fog
is infecting my little black view
of the harbor, so I don't see the fishing ships.
I see the sleep, thief and store.
Thief waiting for the fog to thicken even further.

At That River

last night
I was at sea

and then at the
river, I probably

smelled like
the river.

I moved to Chicago
the insanity

moved right with me
I didn't have my

glasses again
I stayed in a

Salvation Army
rehab, I looked

in the bureau of
glasses they had, they said

find something that
fits. Long before

I used to sleep
on the Mississippi,

I saw so many
sunsets it wasn't

funny. One time
I did time again

because I wanted to
save the fine for

booze. I saved it.
I don't smell

like the river anymore,
but last night I

was at sea, and then
at that river: river

flowed in a cadence,
the story lapped

like the simple
water: rowed with

my glasses, couldn't
understand the woman

and her glasses
in the other raft.

River Sister

So I looked down into the swamp,
the clouds raised their feet
in my small stone, the house walked,
the moon appeared so many times
I said sister, I'd better say sister

because if I don't say sister
I might say love, lid, river—
and then the rope will swing twice
across the swamp, the clouds will
retire to the town on horseback,

—so I say sister and accomplishment,
oh my terror and my pain in travel,
in burning as travel burns, my father
the violin teacher, tapping his father
upon the shoulder—mistake, mistake,

mistake and accomplishment: here is a wind
where my river sister hated me, and I
screamed back, and my brother held
his anger in bottles, voices, daily solitaire
with grandmother, smoke and lies

and me proffered feet for reading by the clouds,
by the tree the old man breathed in
by the reversal of my life
by the hatred of teaching
by all judgments which doom

the house of witchcraft to over there,
to that swamp and that direction, to the years

before you appeared so many times I said your
name built a house around itself and I might
say nothing except I am an error, far white owl

farther in the night when I tapped your shoulder
and hid my face—I have wanted to leave here
for many days to be upon the road to the river you,
having burned my house, traveling within my small stone,
calling lisa, lisa across your name

Murnau

—AFTER THE PAINTING BY WASSILY KANDINSKY

You think of the moon now
as not that bizarre thing,
like the landscape with mountains

it is a simple thing: not wolf, not harvest.
Not candle in a jar.
Not: drawing improved. But the

original one: the one with the markings
of the landscape on the eyes and face.
The nose. The blue picture

which is the moon also.
The buildings between the two of you.
The grid. The grid at twilight

in that so-called bizarre
privacy behind that closed window.
Be calm: the locomotive

churrs its wheels
even in the seen mountains,
seen end.

An end to your weeping
my child. Moon
is a past thing,

gate with shadow,
window with loon:
each cry out on the water

like the original, like the original
nose you drew, like the original
mountain the moon was

before adjectives
like wolf and harvest.
I had a dream

just the other night:
a man from an organization
came to me with my head, my head was

my head and also my penis, there
were boundaries over it,
numbered. He said

God had brought me into this world
to be an example of how insane
insane is. And I thanked the man

and told him I would also
remember a full moon was near.
I want the moon as a simple thing:

when I saw it rising tonight
between the grids
I realized I was bizarre enough,

insane if you will,
without thinking the moon
complicates it.

Maybe I am not even insane.
Maybe this drawing with the markings
(the rain, the box, the poplars)

is insane. I do not think so.
Maybe if I knew if the wolf was blue,
even the harvest was blue,

if these were blue
adjectives for us.
If I brought the original

moon down here to us
(tonight I wondered if the moon
rising in fullness brought

me to my own rising, an ice
memory, some sphere I only
remember in the gut, in the psychic

gut, in the intuitive jar
my body might be)—if I brought the
original moon down to us:

would I see what I was,
would I see my nose,
would the calm candle quietly break

the calm jar? I repeat
myself to get a hold on things:
the moon had a hold on me,

then your drawing, then the simple fact
of simple lunacy in each
coincidence the longing

brings. If the longing
is for you I have brought you
another, I have brought

myself around to a simple
gate and I go in.
It is stark and seen.

Child at Anchor

I needed to turn the faces away—
I was returning
and could not hold the shade from the past life
in the current light, or the lack of the light the shovel
still calls in me, the lack of being
when the prison I made of faces
pulls the shade impossibly low: I am faceless wonder
in that corridor, with my arms crossed against my chest.
Another child is beautiful and walks away
in residual beauty.

I am the same head turned low in a moan,
the scalp of my judgment
gleams like the barber's knife,
the barber I go to has to smile,
the bottles of tonic gleam in the mirror,
gleam even in their old liquid.

Wednesday, Thursday, Friday. A single anchor
rests on the shore. The sky is a drug
where a single drop of light
flies against a mirror behind me, and I turn
and see a single window and a single mirror facing
the shore from the single room the mirror is in,
and a bird in prison—

a brown and black bird with brown and white
beneath its wings—

a single bird in prison flies from the book which is
the water, like a child at anchor
in a prisoner's version
of a prison by the sea.

Eerie

When in my terror I have not given you
the admiration, when I have not felt the rain
chilling my body when it chills my body,
and I have fallen asleep green but in the green light
which is not the illumination the potato light gives off,
which is not the corridor leading to a window
in the middle of the city, in the middle of the room
where the stone drops
but I do not see it.

My face is chipped as I fall.
A breath as heavy as a stone in the cave
closes the lamp at the city's end: then the picture
of the city with a red and yellow boundary
is riddled with bullets, the dream where my aunt and uncle
die off, unseen, diagonally crosses
the morning
like the stroke a blade makes during the wild horse hunt,
like the upside down horse
in the return of the righteous sunlight,

—it is so soon to be so distracted,
too soon to be at the city's feet, images intact,
but the stone dropping.

In the dream there is a white lamp.
Rain inside. A window closing on two roofs.
A visit postponed. The boundary of the sea
and the boundary of the window.

House with a tree in terror.
Another white lamp.
The middle of the city.

I can feel the paradox,
held in the single moment of turning north
when I am turning south. When the illumination
of a negative crosses the dream
or crosses the floor
or crosses the city disguised as a horse.

Disguised at taking everything,
everything
literally.

The rain is on today, the rain is off.
The dream of my aunt and uncle dying off is unseen.

It is the star I cannot see which is so eerie
I may as well be upside down.

Enigma

When I crossed the street I saw my friend differently,
the story of the neck began: for there on his neck
was a purple splotch. How often had he done well with
this splotch: as in: old tale: peering around the door
only when the elves cannot see in return, so you see them,
so you see the night light bathed in yellow, the hand as
the brain, the drawing the door, the window the frame.
Mr. Window: I have properly spent too many years confusing
this splotch with some enigma of the soul: thus one night
when the ghosts were out: I took the porch by the hand
and my love and I went walking. There was no end to this
feeling of the other life: weight of the other life. So
the walk went on and on. Then we came to the river (the
willow river, the river where the water is white at night)
and saw the souls sitting upon the river stones. My friend
with the neck was telling this story: when I crossed the
street I saw my friend differently. He had not departed
as I had thought, not for this world or the next. He stood
and stayed. I had no other choice but to walk away from
him at such a direction so that he might see the splotch
on my neck. The tax of staying put. The other life was
meant to get on . . .

My Cobbler

It was told I could pull
the wagon of death
as long as I chose to pull.
My shoes didn't tell me,
my cobbler told me.

My cobbler tells me a lot of things.

I turned you into a widow,
I was that tough on myself,
the two of us effaced
like stones you might erase

the miles from, the journeys
of the names and other stars
and evenings.

Series of Photographs (The Genus)

This is the one
where my mother
met the night.
My father is tired,
sitting next to
a star from my
childhood.
Where is he?
He does not answer this.
He doesn't ask it.

This is the one
where the street
looks like a train robbery,
the trees are cramped
along the road.
My aunt's farmhouse
is farther up the road,
I don't know why
this was taken.
I think this is my favorite.
I used to walk
through the damp grass.
It was always high,
it was always summer.

Now, almost spring,
I'm looking through
other photographs or cards—
also waiting to know the genus

of the tree outside the small window,
the genus of the dome in the distance
above the southwest roofs, the genus
of that dome before it passes into
a view of oblivion for the trees,
for the trees will bloom—

and looking through those cards
I find various landscapes—none
tropical though—but these landscapes
scrape through as I scrape through,
no here, no intended, no nude
closing the door
or about to close the door.

The room is so small I can
see why I cannot keep finances
in this gift notebook—I have no
finances—why I must return
to the small, why I must see

the nude me, the befriended past
of the real self when the particular
hour was the particular
the way it was as a child.

Maybe there is nothing wrong with
this loneliness I seek, this contemporary
loneliness with a contemporary house,

upon a lonely street in a quiet
quiet village of the city.
Maybe this is even close to why

the man I heard of
troubled himself for not accepting
his negative life, although it was a former life

as far as he could see.
Some days, some parts of days,
this wasn't far at all: he used to visit the city

and always
paid particular homage
to one university street: it appeared foreign,
out of place in a place he would like to be,

a place he wanted to be lonely.
The stones of the street and buildings
were a far-from-loneliness white,
a place he would like to be.

Maybe there is nothing wrong with
this contemporary loneliness: night after day
the house lights go off and the street lights go on,
the evening looks like cardboard.

Negative life begins to feel like an actual negative
held in the hands, held in both hands
as if it were truly a precious thing.

The picture conveyed makes me think of a dead goldfish,
a parent amazed that somehow he "did" this.
The feeling of murder begins to feel

like an actual negative, even if one
doesn't know what the feeling is . . .

but then, we have each murdered, a someone,
a something, a trail, a feeling . . . the details

oddly become less important than the identifying,
major feeling the mark makes.

I open the windows and let night enter the house.
From far off white loneliness settles upon the white page.

I am convinced it is an act against white loneliness
to say so.

The Three of Us Stones

When I was in the harbor
I was at sea.
I haven't seen the sea lately.
I'm in the harbor of the city.

I realized tonight
I haven't seen a stone
in these 5 months.
Not a single
solitary stone.

I've not counted but seen
countless windows,
above ground, below ground,
window upon another form of window.

I'm wondering if the world's population
of stones is decreasing
for even at the harbor
in the sea
I saw no stones,
and no stones
in the countryside town
I was in before that.

Stones, I'm sure, accounted
for this multiplicity of windows,
windows to overcome
the propensity of stones.
Far be it
for the world of windows
to allow the stones
foothold again.

In an old childhood photograph
of stones
my brother my sister and I
are standing. And as my brother
motioned for a stone
in a recent dream

I saw that my entire face
in the photograph
consisted of a concave eyeball,
the length of my face,
the right hemisphere.

Tonight I wrote a letter
from the city
to another city.
I mentioned the dream.
I recalled for the first time
I always motioned
people's eyes to my brother's eyes
when I showed this photograph
of childhood, and stones,
the three of us stones
standing there,—

it is now as if
my brother's eyes—
those beautiful eyes of his
from our childhood of stones—

as if my brother's eyes
allowed my eyes

although I believed none of this
until tonight
when I realized

I have not touched
a single solitary stone.

My brother and my sister and I:
we were beautiful stones.

The Man of Forgiveness

hardly broken
is the echo before
it is a piece,

the boulder in
the sky, the sky
quicker and crying

as a memory of green
starvation upon
the street, stomach

wasted, swollen,
the man of forgiveness
far away he thinks

with his field
and his echo of field.

Untitled

I wanted to love those
I wanted to love, often
I did not want those
who loved me: it was

a disagreement with myself
as if myself was myself,
like trees which are so laden
with night they are night trees,

which they are not. Sometimes
the end is a contradiction
of the tale: the end is simply
not the end, the contradiction

of wanting the end and
not wanting it. I want you.
I no longer want. I wanted
to love those I wanted.

The Laundry Worker

I do laundry.
I work with my mother.
My clothes get stained
by the detergents. My mother's
clothes get stained,
a little less.

So when I go to see Nellie
and John a sheet is out,
over the chair or couch—
my clothes are clean but
stained. And I say I am beautiful,

I am only partially there.
I find: I found: a twenty,
a ring, a slip.
Mother kept the slip.
We can keep anything we find

(anything we find we keep).
I don't have much confidence.
I don't even like the word.

The sea in the town is not so red today.
I'm the only one in town who knows it's red.

The laundry comes off the ship.
The winter's in, the ship sails less.
She is a blue ship on a red sea.

I am thirty five. I look fifty.

That's where the laundry comes from.

Onyx

last october my uncle lester died. his wife, my aunt by blood,
told me to take, keep his onyx ring. i was given a watch often
worn by him also, a very simple watch—no ghost to the watch
and i wore it.
                        i made an omen of the ring. i don't know why—
the blackness
of the stone bothered me, i initially made that into a simple
        sign.
also: a man came to the house of the aged
on the second day of the wake,

seemed to want, my aunt took me aside and said, some other
ring of lester's—a war ring, a service ring, and at the funeral
        home
the same man seemed a little drunk and i sat and watched him
        spend
time over the open casket, almost hunting for
a ring. he didn't get it,
even though he took my uncle's dead hand
and held it like a little wing for a second in his drunkenness.
felt like he was examining the living.

    my aunt always takes me aside
and away to tell me things,
        but i couldn't ask her
about my ring—i was given

a large old family bible too,
with a ledger in the back page

listing the birth and death dates of the ten brothers and sisters
in my mother's family. i took a few deeds too—old land in
   carleton

the family had bought in 1917.

After the second Lisa
I ironed my money
and made the spaces between the dollars
glow. And like the dark underground

and the darkness of the underground
I glowed there
with obsession
for another batch of money,

for another batch of names,
and I heard my father
and the father inside him
repeat your name also,

and I was confused.
My father handled money all his life
just like I handle names,
my ironing attracts the exacting petty attention

I never weighed, and so careless
in my weighing the money has altered,
the name has gone,
the neighbors use the second sunlight

in order to peer directly in:
I now distinguish the ashes from the hearts,
the horses from the donkeys,
the sequel from the non sequitur.

And like the sunlight
the second name has a second life,

her money is darkness,
her ashes are lame

like the sequence of the horses,
the sequence in which the orphaned horse
grew lamer as the orphaned horse's
suffering was not discussed

by the more major horses, those horses
who had seen and experienced
the beatings, the maiming, the winter nights
when the souls of dollars

flapped their ugly wings,
and the horses flew under them as they flew
driven from a fire, while miles away the fleeing
horses glowed in the central fire

of someone's clothing,
someone like my father at the bank,
someone like the second name
who was glowing.

Too Many Drops

I died when I gave her
the rose, hadn't ever
felt so gravely dead.
Warren—the brother—
resented me, tore
the rose (or so she said).

The house of the dead
is a mile long with candles:
the moon is out
but they don't talk about the moon.

The marble I named doug
has been dead at least 29 years,
maybe a few more. I had
all the other marbles in a circle
for a funeral, just west
of the register, the point
of doug's disappearance.

And Pricey's been dead
a long time—though I heard
him with me one hallucinogenic
afternoon in a dune shack.

And all those people
I took for comfort—
what a joke it seems now,
the white and the black
of the past, not dropped off
yet—and all this I have seen lately
about the drop,—

the moon will drop in another thousand years
the planet earth may drop before
my penguin drops whenever I kid him
about the crow flying
and all of us live a life of comparison.

Even on a starkly cold night with a moon
staring from whiteness
the house of the dead falls asleep
much more slowly than most houses.

Too many stories being told, too many disappearances,
too many drops.

The Bicycle

I took about 8 long slow rides:
one street was as it turned out
a bend: a man with a very unsouthern
name on his mailbox was standing
in his small back yard with another
man: the grill was firing and they
were holding a beer. The entire
bend was a series of small small
box houses: white populace: looked
like poor white. The fact that got me
was in front and in some cases the
back of each were huge tall trees,
obviously they built the boxes
but decided to keep these small
touches called tall trees. The lawns
were pine needles and didn't look
bad. On the other side of the bend
I took a look in the very unsouthern
name's backyard and saw the two of
them from behind: still standing.
I don't know if I could stand still
in that neighborhood that long: they
have, the trees have, the houses
don't so much stand as they just are:
white box, brown box, white box:
once in awhile there is an odd one
obviously older that has an extra
room or a garage.

83 Grade School Children

for William and Susan

There are very few unqualified smiles
in the photograph, a few are looking off
as if a dog is barking
beside the photographer, or a
flower is telling them to divide
their attentions already, so that preparation
for life other than family life
may always beckon. The boy
standing out in front looks to me
like a version of Rusty, who befriended
me in "my" school, miles and miles away
from this one. The fact is
at least a third of these faces
looks like fatter or slimmer versions
of the children I was among—
in some cases it seems just a matter of
moving a cowlick slightly left,
or removing the glasses.

As the Five

When the world is way ahead of me
I want to kiss my sister: punch me, my shista,
kiss me too: I have found a sunset for us

which for six evenings running
is just like the cover of our book,
the one we shared before tearing it to shreds:

look, six birds alight,
the globe turns still without them in a tree,
they alight again from the very sky

one looking
like it isn't the same species as the five:
weddings begin with fables

such as this:
lawd, lawd, we don't know.

The Time

There is this long discussion of tragedy
and the end is in sight: what will I do,
I will be good at that sea, another weight,
another sea. As horrible as the stars are

they are outrageous, in their little fledgling lights
in their sea, the sea of night and the sea
of the rages, the wages which are not yours
or mine or any hill belonging to anyone under

the same raging night. But the time, the time
when the weight drops from the light, kisses
the hill with the fact of its light across
same seas of night: the wages of tragedy,

the pathetic ego hanging in the light, the sea
there, the hill, all the time turned back
by the little gas in the little preposterous
lamp of the ego.

The Autobiography of a Suicide

I believed in God but God abandoned me for someone.
One part of my life remained uncontrived: conversations
about God, which as few and far between as they were
the conversations contrived to reach others in a
location they could call the future, the strangers
and lack of fluency they all begged for, each with
a common sitting-duck-of-a-soul, windowed against
windows, stones, the buildings I call stones unless
they consist of wood and string: the stuff children's
memories compose against a dark moon when the mother
and father return late as mine did, due to snow, due
to extended family, due to darkness the moon hid from us.
I believed in God only because we all spoke the same
language. I can't give you examples at this late date:
suffice to say the past and the future were among the
incidents, and the awful detail of me handing a mask of
my face to my friend, almost as if it was time for him
to don the mask, any mask, mine or not. But it was my
dream and therefore I suppose why it was my mask. This
is only one of the many things the dream could mean or
point to. I like the life that just points. I know there
will be moments when I will regain the starry examples
the sea sets and there will be moments when I will lose
this.

The Autobiography of Talullah Bankh

The woman said she was
sick in bed when she
perused it—but the photographs
gleamed from the rainy pages
on a cloudy night—

there was the mountain range,
that was an old one, out
somewhere west, hung upon
the family wall over
the family fireplace

—all was family,
family ending. The photograph
of the aging—a constant river
eating the banks,

but rivers have done so
for a thousand years anyway:
and where are they now,
the old ones, the mountains
or the rivers or the aging

loneliness under the
stark night cutting along
the river's glow where
the edge creeps in:

childhood, a thousand stars,
the nights by the family
when the lights cut the
mountain and the river

in half: life now
life later, o endless
parade of life
in the photograph of rained

loneliness. It rained briefly,
it fell briefly. The family
overheard their stories one
more time. It rained.

They listened finally.
The photograph of the mountain
beckoned like
light might

upon the morning vase—one
overhears the family
in the vase,
the story continues.

three

1985–1986

don't believe in the death anymore
just the place of it / one geography
with a road and snow

one death to begin all death
it is small and is among the river
the rock and the tree / it remembers

me before I do
and that's no small affair:
for the rock and the river

remember death for me
the tree wants to but is a
part of nature which must be

restrained / it is a
sympathetic restraint among
the voices the roads and the snow

it remembers best
the place of death it did not
remember anymore

"On a Train Approaching Midnight"
—AFTER A LINE BY LOUIS SIMPSON

On a train approaching midnight
I lost my copy of Gide's *White Notebook.*
It was given as a gift, inscribed.
The loss of this gift preceded the loss of her
by five days.

On a train approaching midnight
the younger man of the two requested
we sit in the rear of the car to talk.
I became his confidant. It was a boring
story. The car was so empty we wouldn't
have needed to retreat that far. The other
slept. The story was so blinding I could see
only our own reflection in the glass.

On a train approaching midnight
two loves sleep. One is dreaming
of a snowy novel, one one will choose.
One one will read in peace and privacy
in a country of snow which forbids
personal reading. The other is dreaming
of a slightly oversized tarot deck, designed
in braille, is fingering the deck like a coin.
Trees are lashing at rain outside. The night
is rain on a train approaching midnight.

At the God Hour

Gogol (his namesake) felt inordinate distances,
lonely ones,

whenever he and his love
were in the company of almost anyone, even their families.

If ghosts were possible
birds would walk only at twilight,

at the god hour
which descends like a plausible sun

traveling in the wrong direction.
And it isn't necessarily

lonely when the sun goes down
and the darkness comes upon that white house

near the large cold stone
with snow coming down in the countryside

and only one light on.
It's not a very complete light.

Wouldn't it make a lot more sense
if Gogol and his love just let everybody be?

The train whistles.
3 units of signals, red signals, shine briefly in the night.

Ivan Akaky
(The Crossing of Two Stories)

The memory is her memory,
she's mistaken the name,
the story. She believes
the story is a rhapsodic violet,
portrait of a stolen man,
a stolen coat, a man
of two cities whose wedding mask
is a sea of blackbirds—

blackbirds which in the night
will avenge his death,
will avenge those lonely,
starving, exchanged.
The memory is her memory.
The name is Gogol's
Ivan Shponka, suffocated
into marriage, at least
the story suggests
this doom, leaning
in a description of his dreams
like a fever, like a bell from which
the moon must climb

every night
in order to light part
of a night world
except when it is new and can afford
no light. Except
when it is somnambulistic,
lost in a closer space,
only audible to those

who trace the daily moon
like a religion. Ivan Fyodorovich Shponka
has gone to sleep,
if that fever could be fairly
called sleep,
the poor soul
is shallow and clear
like a brook, if only

the sound of kisses could replace
the bell which tolls so finally,
the shoulder of a wounded bird
is such a precise bell

it dwarfs the ringing, jangling
of the sleigh bells
across the other fever
in her memory where she has confused
Akaky with Ivan—

Akaky, face without an alibi,
Akaky, robbed of his overcoat
the ghastly fever
of snow falling . . .
idiot snow . . .

the night is streaked
with sounds of rain and wind
outside her window,
the streaking of the sounds
upon her house is as if

the night for once misspells
its sounds: the roof is the rain,

the window is the wind,
a branch against a shutter
(or is it just the shutter)
is a broken cup from a distant shelf—

nearing the deepest moment
of night, moment which one
can never completely trace,
she dreams for the second time
in her life of handing a mask
to her lifelong friend,

they are upon a train
and passing another village
in which another bell tolls.

Snow is falling.
The mask is morose.

In order to protect her friend
she has within the dream
changed the sex of the face
of the friend,

across the distance of the deepest moment
which is as close as her bed to a window
she and friend
sit comfortably apart

while the train stops
to take on more passengers.

The night is as alone as Akaky,
this too the dream perceives.
The night is just as alone . . .

The Night Is a Sea

One evening on the farm a woman decides to reclaim her life. The night is not as much of a moment as it seems: she remembers a sky from three years ago, she sang to it, the river did not so much accompany her song that night as did the silence of the river.

When she finds herself in the world she's seeking red shoes. A dream is loud with them. She wears the red shoes and boards a train to another city.

The ring she is wearing is like a city. At the edge of the city there's an orchard of pear trees and silent night. She meets a man and another man. The "another" man has been foreshadowed by the town at night, the song she sang, a lamp across a road.

The train is climbing in a line of white. The steam is like the world, it is always drifting back, always an accompaniment, always the history of masses reduced for a moment only to the history of one, or two.

They keep riding higher, letting people in, letting people off.

A star streaks across the night like a moment in the history of a shoe.

The night is a sea, their life is a shore, the train is the minute but vast boundary of the two.

Guatemala

Only the military
can try the military.
So far they've shown
little inclination to do so . . .

dismembered:
Beatrice, hands off, slashes everywhere
across from the heart.
Her corpse is
a star, a sea, a hand which will come back:

some major's clock will be turned back
and awaking to repair it
he will be mortally wounded by
a star, a sea, a hand which will come back:

a tongue from some colonel's boot will fall off
and bending to retrieve it
he will be mortally wounded by
a star, a sea, a hand which will come back:

a card from some general's deck will be missing
and taking this out on an Indian
he will be mortally wounded by
a star, a sea, a hand which will come back:

tonight driving back from a meeting
I drove the alley as the trees in the night snow beckoned

—the lights were out in the house I was born in
and for the first time ever it felt as if

someone from that house had lived
and someone from that house had died.

The Gambler

He is deadheading on the train to Buffalo.
He glances at the sun across the snow
and his hands and across the snow again.
He glances as far as Amsterdam and then closes his eyes
and sees his life:

a sameness, a long world of don't,
a broken road and an awful lot of traveling,
and a sigh for no one,
not anyone at all, a gambler's sigh which
draws another sigh, and another.

No one.
Hands placed in a dream upon countryside.
No one's.
Deadheading on a train to Buffalo
for the hundreth hundreth time.

Who in his right mind
would hold the brothers
to blame?
They lived in their own
mental torment,
unrelieved by day
or their own lies.

The sun dropped like a stone one night
and the brothers talked on.
The past, the son, the younger people
in their life. The garden.

The heart can approach the day
as if the day is a stone.
The sun has risen. The stone
has risen. One wants what one wants.
One foolishly insists one wants
the stone. It is a weight
unrelieved, but one is sure
one can handle the stone.

The weight drops
like a shovel piercing
the garden. The moon
is so heavy the brothers
would like to pierce it.
Night is out,
stark night.

Zane Grey

named in books
named songs in pictures

I have no desire to be this green wood.
I have chosen this name in order to be free.
It has always tasted, this name, it has always felt like an actual
  thing.

When I was a child I was surrounded by green wood.
The delusion existed: time would stand still.
It seemed to particularly stay still Friday evening and Friday
  night.
The entire world did not exist beyond green wood.
When it rained on those Fridays
the smell of forever filled the night air as green wood.

They insert a real Tube into the painted wound

What a prison,
this evening, this night, this wood, this lack of the sun
and anyone else. For no one entered this world
except those named in books, songs, pictures.
The one picture we always avoided was a man waking in the
  night
with the devil after him and it was simply called "Death."
There was one part of one song I always tried skipping over
for it contained a narrative portion in which a man contracted
  fever
and an eerie flute noted the fever.
I haunted me.

One neighbor knocked on the door of the green wood one
  Friday night,
it was raining, and although a very grown man he called me, a
  child,
a coward for not entering the night with him.

There were joyous parts to this green wood: a warmth, a
     touching, a quiet
communication as if we all silently preferred this slight lack of
     light and did not ever
want to depart from one another.

Of course we had to depart for time did not stand still.
The world of green wood lasted only another year or so from
     the time I was first
able to perceive it.

The Beautiful Hand

for Susan Lyman

He had walked into the room unreal.
He was sure he was. The major window
faced the sea
another—smaller and in back—the street.

He spent three days facing through the sea,
it felt like that,
and he chose the street: the view felt darker,
cut-off, confined. He was used to that and he could take it.
He wasn't actually wrong
but he didn't do so well back there.
Only on days it rained and he could tell
the trees were wet
and therefore part of the world felt wet.

Between these two
was a loft where they slept, the sea could
still be seen but from above
and slightly. Wonderfully he could look to
the sky above the street and a chimney
went straight through the loft and he liked that.
Here he stayed for about an hour.
No, it would not work, it was very simply
too good to be true, too high a view
of sea and sky for anyone like him.

A year passed before he left as he came, unreal.
One night, in the middle of the year, he wept in bed
after reading old attempts of his at stories
and a beautifully written story by someone else
—a woman—which ended with the dying of a deer.

It wasn't because his stories were good he wept,
it was simply because they were.

They had been.
And as much as the deer died
he wept at the beautiful hand which did the telling.

For himself,
for the life beside him.

To K. and S.

Between Utica and Amsterdam there's an old
folks home. It is its own compound,
they have a few barns and even have
graves, neat rows of stones, about 50.
I assume the dead old folks are buried there.
There's nothing on the surrounding hills but
trees and the hills are steep. I used to
wonder what it would be like to have to escape
from there, who has the keys, are the old ones
in willingly or not. I've also had an urge to imagine the place
as a resort, keeping its history as an old folks
home for a drawing card for tourists or artists who
would enjoy painting landscapes and stones in the summer.

A little farther down the line is an admirable
horse farm: it has a bridge and the creek tends to
make the boundary. The main house is a clean 4 storeys:
you can see right on through as the place is
vacated. Even from the train I could tell there wasn't
a stick of furniture in the place. We would like it in the winter
and we could leave when the people came.

There were two murders in my hometown this week.
One ended on a dead end road—the road's an end
only in the winter because of snow. They theorize a chase:
man caught in act of theft, takes owner's gun, is chased
across county into Herkimer, owner doesn't know thief has his
gun. Thief is unfamiliar with fact of dead end road in
winter. Owner has scribbled license number of car he's
    chasing.

Police find number on car seat with dog, who is left alive
inside.

The other is a card game, enough to make you sick.
Two men meet in unnamed bar (police refuse to name it),
return to younger one's apartment and the older one by 4 a.m.
    has
lost $200 bucks to the young one and the cards. They argue
and the loser is stabbed not once or twice but often.
It all takes place over my old barber shop, "Malone's."
At 9 a.m. an unnamed source walks into the police
and says there's been a murder and a few moments later an
    unnamed
caller calls and tells the cops where the young one is.
The young one is picked up without resistance "somewhere"
in the 100's of East Bloomfield. He's 22 and the father of 3
pre-school children. He lived in the 5 room apartment above
    "Malone's"
alone.

Twice on this train I've walked by a man who looks like Jake
    M. of my
distant past. His buddy Anthony fat but tough wanted to beat
    up on
me one night when a bunch of us attended a stupid Catholic
    League
football game. The last I knew Jake M. owned a liquor store.
The hometown wrote it up in the local paper.
It's a daily sentinel and it stinks.

To J.

Do you remember?

—Would you worry?

Do you?

Tomas says the houses know very much what they're doing—
there's a deliberate quality of the sun to them
even in their darkest hours. One must look to see it
but the deliberate quality of the sun is there.

I remember trying to write Tomas a few years ago. I wanted
to tell him of a recurring train dream. The tracks were beside a
    lake
but there were dunes as if the lake was really a sea. I rode in a
    small open coach.
The conductors always had something friendly but odd to say
    to me.
"If you face this way you can return to your past."
"Today there is fog on the lake, just like your life."

I was drinking heavily. Most people were off to work,
my friend was, and I was already drinking heavily.
A few lines into the letter I didn't even know what I was
    saying.
I'm staying at my friend's apartment drunk again
at 9 a.m.

—I think we're very hard on ourselves, even now.
I always hear this in others.
The sun has some preoccupation with our destiny,

it's almost as if we don't want to look that way,
or can't bear to, or believe.

That was one sense I had of the messenger,
that the messenger said "believe."

One time I wanted to leave in an envelope
a paper containing all my desires. I would confer with it
every few years to see how close I'd come.
They would have been listed simply—sea, stars, singing—
I have this feeling now
singing erases the acts of the past
as the song becomes so much its own act.
Writing never quite did that, the past
didn't become transparent enough in writing. Song just seems
    to say

yes
I am doing this, I am doing that, I have done.
I am traveling across a snowy countryside, on a train,
to see friends. I see the houses and the fields,
some are living and some are dead.
I would like to be traveling to the sea
instead of the metropolis
but this will more than do.
I have done.

There: an old bridge
where they've taken the bridge away on each side
you could go as far as the river but not across it.

I don't think a song would ever do that,
take the bridge away from a bridge.

—Do you remember if the train ever stopped in the dream?

Yes. It went the distance of the lake, turned and returned.

—Somehow I didn't think a train in a dream would have a
  destination.

Cast Any Shadow

Many prisons: the literal concrete ones,
the barbed ones,
the prison which does its utmost to guarantee
you won't breathe, sleep, sing—
and it feeds you the infested.

The head ones, and perhaps these are constructed also
around the heart: the visions, voices, none of which
are there except in a space which has become a horrendous
    "mine,"
possessions in
a world of the dispossessed.

A woods
when in flight. A small woods.
The dogs are so sharp you hear the dogs in the leaves.

A house
when in flight. The size of the house doesn't matter. It
doesn't even have to be a house. The hole is inside. It is "mine."

A human portion of the world as legitimate enemy.

Flight
in flight. Birds which fly away from the self.

Last night I saw a couple embrace.
She had driven up to meet him at his bus.
They held each other so tightly I thought the world would fall
    off.

Exit or Death / Fallen Snow

/ fallen bird:

family bird. It is difficult to find the lamp
but the lamp is finally lit. When I wrote that the man found his
    own head sadly

I meant
as John might mean

heart is too often divided from the head
so there is little but head, heart perhaps located momentarily

but with a relative silence or kept silent.
Not always, but often enough. Night belief breathes as a
    system in which one

is absolutely convinced one belongs and then at that very
    moment
falls in the night: a lamp falls, a bird falls

silent to the human ear
the family falls with a huge din. I do not know where to go

in the human night so much as I know
I am there / the birds are there above the fallen snow

having leaned in their tender mockery for me, for you, for
the families which momentarily lean into exit or death

—little remains of us except the family bird which flies against
    the sun
and the song. There's a bold declaration in an ancient meaning

that the bird alights for the lamp, the house, the fallen snow.
    Even night belief
cannot overwhelm the birthright of the family bird. The cage is
    gone /

the cage was always gone. There is even a bird
which leads the snow in falling.

Hawkins Falls

Ginny's dad (visitor: bacon)
Car at lake (cranes)

Reversal of
'81:
Georgie's ghost
Georgie's house / cottage

Where are the clouds?
The ghosts rise, you may rise with them.

So now you've suffered a dream in which you attempt to keep
    me from breathing.
You are no more responsible for the dream than you are for the
    bridge.

The father seemed to wear his heart on his face.
Their friend could not eat bacon because of a recent heart
    attack.

I don't know if they were cranes or loons. Loon Lake was still a
    good 30 miles from us.
So: it was cranes which she whispered for me to see and we
    walked along the lake trail
—I'm carrying her hypo-dermic in case she is stung by a bee.

1981 was upside down: I had entered the cottage / house of the
    childhood ghost
I read of / witnessed in a book years, years back.
    However: I betrayed myself, for this was no reason for me to
        live upside down,
        it wasn't justification,

nor could it become so.
I frequently left town on a bus.

One day I called long distance
and the dog had died. The ghost had stolen an anchor.

I helplessly anchored in the fewer suns
so lost as to be forsaken.

A Fire in the Alphabet

for Z

Where would you go, my
little overlooked one:
labeled from birth
as "the end"—the finish,
the last. Where would you

perish when even the forest
had escaped with each of its
trees and leaves
and even, at the last second,
its worms.

Where o where
would the star look down to see you turning back

to z, small z,
your little sister who in most diagrams
was more belated
than you:

it wasn't that you or she
was ever really late
but that you were branded so, branded as the name is branded
on a boat, a distant friend you talked with once

because of a printer's mistake.
I will bless that printer for you, I promise now

to make enough of an end which no one will brand as nothing,
or a last gasp. A final street upon which the two infamous
    lovers
will fail to clarify themselves until your breath of *z*

briefly and almost invisibly enlightens their language.
And they will leave the street aided at last. And someday
when they are again inattentive I will see if I can seek the
   moon

—that pancake we call the evening grail—
I will see if I can seek the moon to rise momentarily
in your crooked shape,

like a crooked arrow
among the mysteries of the mountains and the seas—
in honor of your patience and brevity.

In honor of extinguishing a fire in the alphabet.

I must believe in love at this moment,
as I say goodbye. I must believe

in the fire for myself, for if I don't believe
for myself
who shall?

I miss you already.
A forest is crying in the stars.

PS: I named my Aunt Dorothy's cat Zania.
No one else ever called her that.

Breathless Storm

10:30. A long and thin
railway building's
been converted into an
antique shop. Snow's

predicted. There are 7
chimneys she can count
from looking southwest
from the hotel window,

only 2 if she sits to
look southeast. No one
is coming. There is a
"Beware of the Dog"

sign on a shed and
she thinks, unfairly,
of herself when she
reads this and stares

upon it. Life is not
so much reflection
she reflects as a
study in resistance,

yours, mine, and the
random scope of all
the other lives out
there which also,

it seems, find their
way to studies

in insistence too.
The screams, the fortunes,

the meanderings of the
life in its ordinary
branches, tributaries
that someone else

conveniently pees upon.
Oh well. I am
excited by the prospect
of traveling alone

to Nova Scotia,
Canada, home of
my mother's birth,
for I have never

seen it in winter.
But I will not go
there feeling like this,
no, I will not knock

upon my sister's door
upon the way there
nor my mother's sister's
door on Crescent Ave.

I will see them instead
in another life, where

the moon wanes there
as well and the sun

waxes hot in summer
and the solstice and
equinox are demarcations
even in a land called heaven.

No, the angel
is of the north wind.
It has a boy's head
and the body of a river
under a street lamp.

When you climb into the sky
the angel will take crow's wings
and make a sentence
from your life.

One bridge.
One angel to each.
The people's faces
are waxed at night
so they may better share
each other's angel.

No, the city hasn't changed
in a thousand years.
As assinine as it may sound
even each city has an angel,
keeping watch on the sad cases
as the city may be.

As those two
at a rendevous
which has never transpired

except in the ledger
of lost causes, hearts
blown, lanes closed.

The Moment of Memory

What can I say of the house now that the house
is over—what can I sing of the bridge
now that my family is on the other side,
where the birds finally tune the shadows
with their songs, and the lights need only
brighten for a moment, for there is no darkness
in their house, only light, the causes of
light, the moment of memory when the
past pronounces the future, "so long," the leaves
wave, the sea waits for someone and someone
else, the night is no longer poor, and the face
of the moon and the face of the sun can now
turn away to the space which is endless for
a moment and another moment more. I love
you for the wing which is white, yellow, black,
for the eye which is nowhere, for the river which
slackens where the sun met it once upon a time
when the world was alive with our song, heeded
the song, the murmur of the place, heart, house,
stars which never burned for we are learning
our song from them and burning would interfere.
It is the beginning and the end of time. You are
within me. I can tell the river and the stars.

oved One

Could be the mild
end of the river
is what I'm looking for

Some mornings when the lagoon
almost reflects the light   _mirror_

some bitch of a memory
bitchess in green

Could be the child
who lived by his wits

Some mornings when the lamp
almost reflects his wits

some bastard called a village
where all they did was pay shame with their lives
professional shame

Don't tell me any more stories of your goddamn trip to Italy
Sooner / later
who cares?

Help me, or read now the letters
I receive from others. It's
a feeling, asking / someone
like you to see them:

I befriended such jerks then
the lonely stare of a lonely house

: autumn. This was the worst season.
The ghosts became a drugged affair,

the evening felt like a clamp
I had a mania for making mistakes and kept saying
yes
yes

I found your face and everyone
looked briefly at the exposed light
before turning toward the open
frame where the loved one sat
forward on the rocks

and the light reflected
anonymous deaths in the village

: I wish

No one out there would believe
the nights I didn't sleep
the nights I set fire
the descending lack of breath

alas, ex-ones,
in here I am believed

at times I even climb
my mother's love

and address the endless committee
of the evening

I even apply
her personal spirit
so I may not spook the deer

A Series of Judgments

Snow is irrational
and the rare song above the snow insane.

Every tree is a personality:
each ticks in the night like a human clock.

It is as uncomfortable to own more than one clock
as it is to own one's name.

Why haven't more tellers robbed banks?
How come there are so many banks?

My brother passes judgment upon me
in dreams he has. One involved a bank.

I know that more than one question is being asked in the city
in the deep middle of the night. I never hear the questions

but they are out there being asked.
A question's only secret is to ask.

When I kissed him I was trying to take the whole thing back.
I knew it was time to leave when the dream kissed me:

the past is no longer damaged goods. The night sky is bright
    with its own dark.
The train you and I have heard

is our train. That is our secret.
A secret we share but a secret nevertheless.

To Rose

If you ever wanted to argue about the end
tonight would be a night for it: the sky has amnesia,

rain falls as ice, the gods must be through with us.
Too many secrets, too many ends:

too many houses of the dead
and the begotten dead.

The influences of the planets,
the seas, the apparition which chooses indigo rain

—only a first love
would choose indigo rain. The end

in indigo, the stillness eating the light of the stillness,
the apparition itself suffering from an amnesia, an amnesia

the end can only near,
can only shadow—out there where one day becomes one night,

one bell tolls so loudly a light comes on in someone's sleep
and she asks another question of the end.

If it is possibly true, a version of the truth,
that a secret is simply another ego structure, then the fool

is such a structure as well, the mask of the fool,
the small closed room in which the fool has confided for so
    long.

A secret is like a version of the world:
a whispered ending shadowing the real, the rock, the sea

the things of this world
which need no apparition.

Too many secrets for the gods to be through with us.
Too much they do not know.

The sea may not need an apparition
—I do.

Someone's sleep begins to feel like a chimney.
And I hear this fire and I wonder how close it will get.

I do not know
mother
if I do fly
what I shall see:

maybe I will fly
above the moon
or to what seems
like the right of

the sun: how often
have we not
said these things
in a conspiracy

of silence
which afflicted
all of us.
It is unaccountable

: whenever I have
questioned it it
has beaten the
shit out of me

I have wanted to
walk near the lake
where we once
lived and understand

why the whole
became ominous so

young. Whenever
I just leave

the conspiracy alone
it remains
unaccountable with
even a tinge of

wonder like how
did we get here
in the first place.
I wanted to tell

you that I am
aging too
you are not
alone—trees

I would like to
walk you past the
old ones for many
of them are still

and you might
recognize some very
much very
clearly. If I

do fly above the
moon I will say

a wish for you and
father. I

may ask if some
moonlight piece
discover you
once more.

It must have
once touched
you and father
or the sun

did. It may
even account
in part for this
long silence though

my guess is that
is our doing or
what doing did to
us. Far be it

from the sun and
the moon
far be it for
the sun and moon

not to help us.
It is never too
late. They too
are old ones.

The World at Dusk

for Charlie Bagley

There are those I attempt to describe.
The words always fail.
One man has a face of winter
and only summer words find me.
Or worse: the words of spring which trample the winter face.

It is not as romantic as a curse.
I find my first two names in a cemetery.
Every moment life is slowly drawing to a close.
One day I will find the third name as well.
I do not know the third name, only that I will find it, or it me.

Anyone is a red house
against the glowing dark.
There are the variations of anyone in the light,
in the form of the house against the landscape,
until the final light is so much it is almost house against
    house.

I see and hear most clearly through other people.
Without them I become almost a solitude.
A place of emptiness.
Perhaps I have needed this emptiness more than I have
    admitted,
perhaps I feared its place for fear of itself.

After thirty nine years I am still
a stranger to myself. I feel exhausted
—living with this stranger for so long.
I do not know what to do with him or for him.
I ask the silence for help.

Help for each of us. For the stranger
also does not know me, and he too must find it odd
to hear his stranger saying "I do not know what to do . . ."
To hear the word help
muttered so closely and not addressed to him.

A Note about the Author

MICHAEL BURKARD was born in Rome, New York, in 1947. He received a B.A. from Hobart College and an M.F.A. from the University of Iowa. Between these degrees he worked as a psychiatric aide and began publishing in magazines in 1970. His books include *The Fires They Kept* (Metro Book Co., 1986), *Ruby for Grief* (University of Pittsburgh Press, 1981), *None, River* (Ironwood Press, 1979), and *In a White Light* (L'Epervier Press, 1977). He received the Alice Fay di Castagnola Award from The Poetry Society of America in 1984, and in 1985 was awarded a grant in poetry from the National Endowment for the Arts. For two years he was a writing fellow at the Fine Arts Work Center at Provincetown. He has taught at various colleges and universities, including the University of Iowa, St. Lawrence University, Kirkland College, Salisbury State College, Syracuse University, and Sarah Lawrence College. He is married to the painter Mary Alice Johnston.